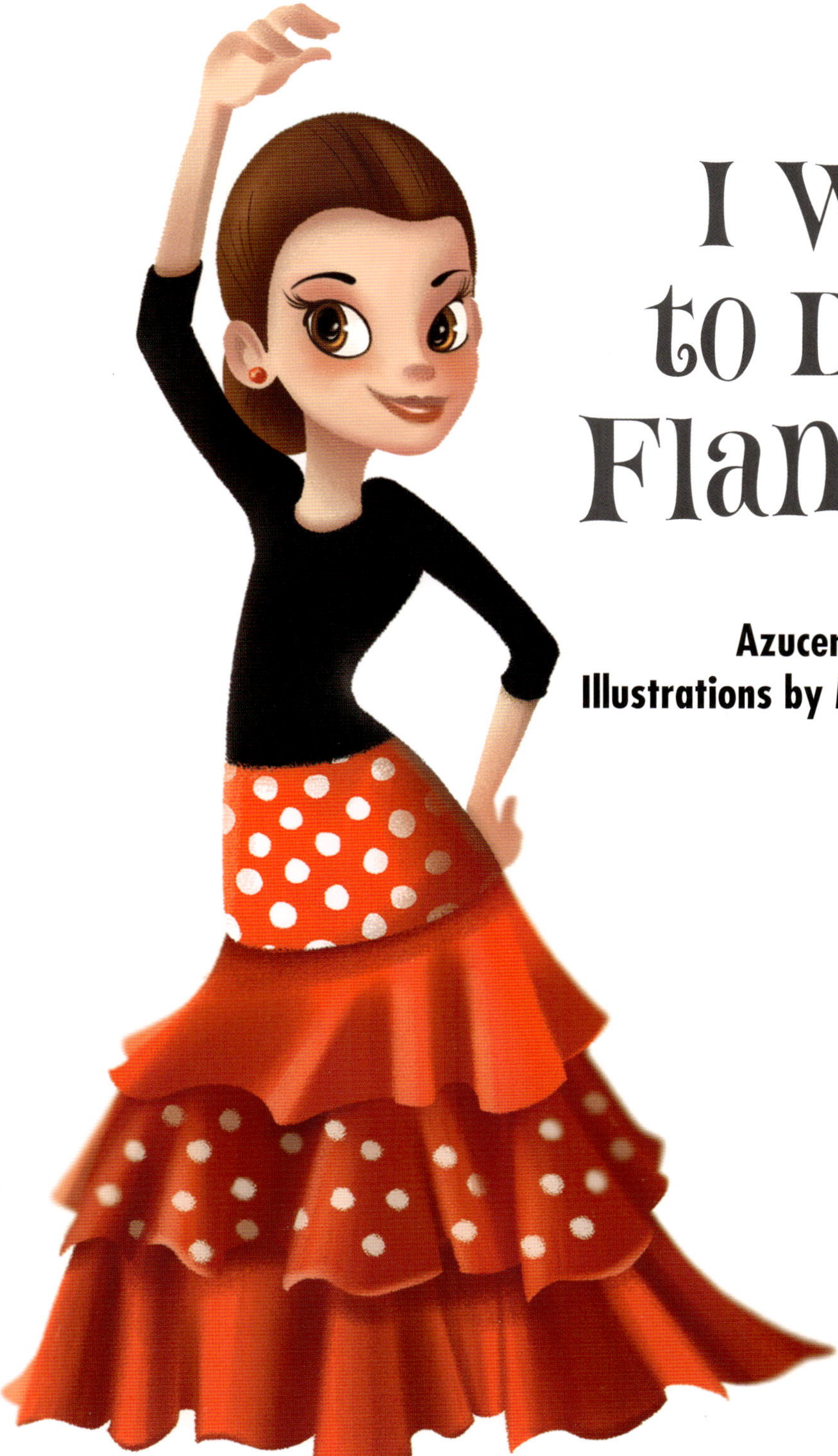

I Want to Dance Flamenco

Azucena Huidobro
Illustrations by Mario García Arévalo

ONIRO

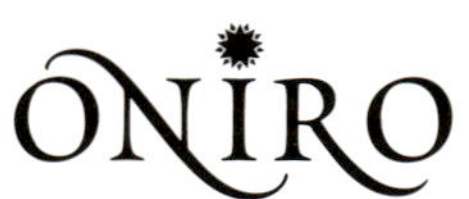

To my parents, thank you! For so much… for everything…
To Carlos and Rocío, because you are my strength and inspiration.
And to all of those, who in one way or another take care of, enjoy and love dance.

ONIRO
Avda. Diagonal, 662-664,08034 Barcelona
www.planetadelibrosinfantilyjuvenil.com
ww.planetadelibros.com

First edition: May 2014
Third edition: February 2017
ISBN 978-84-9754-746-8
Depósito legal: B. 1.652-2014
Printed in China

The paper used in this printing is one hundred percent chlorine free and qualified as ecological.

HI! My name is SARA and one of the things I like the most in this world is to DANCE.
It doesn't matter where I am, when I listen to music, my feet get going...
For some time, I have been going to a dance school. And I'm learning how to dance FLAMENCO! I LOVE IT!
I learn a lot of things, and even though some of them are not easy at all, I make an effort and have a great time.

THE WORLD OF FLAMENCO IS SO THRILLING, MAGICAL AND FILLED WITH SECRETS...

DO YOU WANT TO DISCOVER THEM WITH ME?

I was only 3 years old, when I got my first Flamenco shoes. I wanted to wear them all day long... I ADORED THEM!
A year later, my parents sent me to a dance school for lessons. On my first day, I walked in a bit nervous with my skirt and heels, and found a lot of other girls like me: who enjoyed dance and were dying to learn!

AND THAT'S HOW IT ALL BEGAN...!

Flamenco is thrilling! it has a lot of strength; it is very expressive and oozes feeling. It's hard to explain, but when you like flamenco, you feel it inside, because it comes straight from the heart.

PLAY IT,

YOU CAN SING IT,

DANCE IT...

and above all, FEEL IT!

Ole

FLAMENCO COSTUMES

In the beginning, maybe you'll just have a skirt for classes and your first shows... But, don't worry, soon you'll see yourself dressed with a gorgeous Flamenco gown!

Besides, you can adorn it with shawls, earrings, bracelets... and of course, flowers and back comb your hair!

PIECE OF ADVICE!

Put your accessories on well, so they won't disturb you while you dance.

The train gown is the queen of all stages!

It's a gown that ends with a long train surrounded by ruffles.

It's elegant, majestic and very, very SPECTACULAR! It's hard to manoeuvre. You need a lot, and I mean a lot of practice to learn the technique of moving it correctly.

FLAMENCO SHOES

Are you ready to use your feet as instruments? You are going to hit the floor following the beat with your sole or your heel. This is called «zapatear,» or shoeing, one of the most showy Flamenco techniques.

So, you'll need a special pair of shoes so you can «zapatear», or do music with your feet, without hurting yourself! Your first pair will be simple, but later on, you'll have ones with reinforcements on the toecap and nails in the tip and the heel.

That way, «zapatear» or shoeing, sounds better!

THE CASTANETS

I'm learning how to play the castanets and it's a lot of fun!
Even though they look so simple, they are such and amazing instrument.
You make with them very special sounds with overtones and unique nuances!

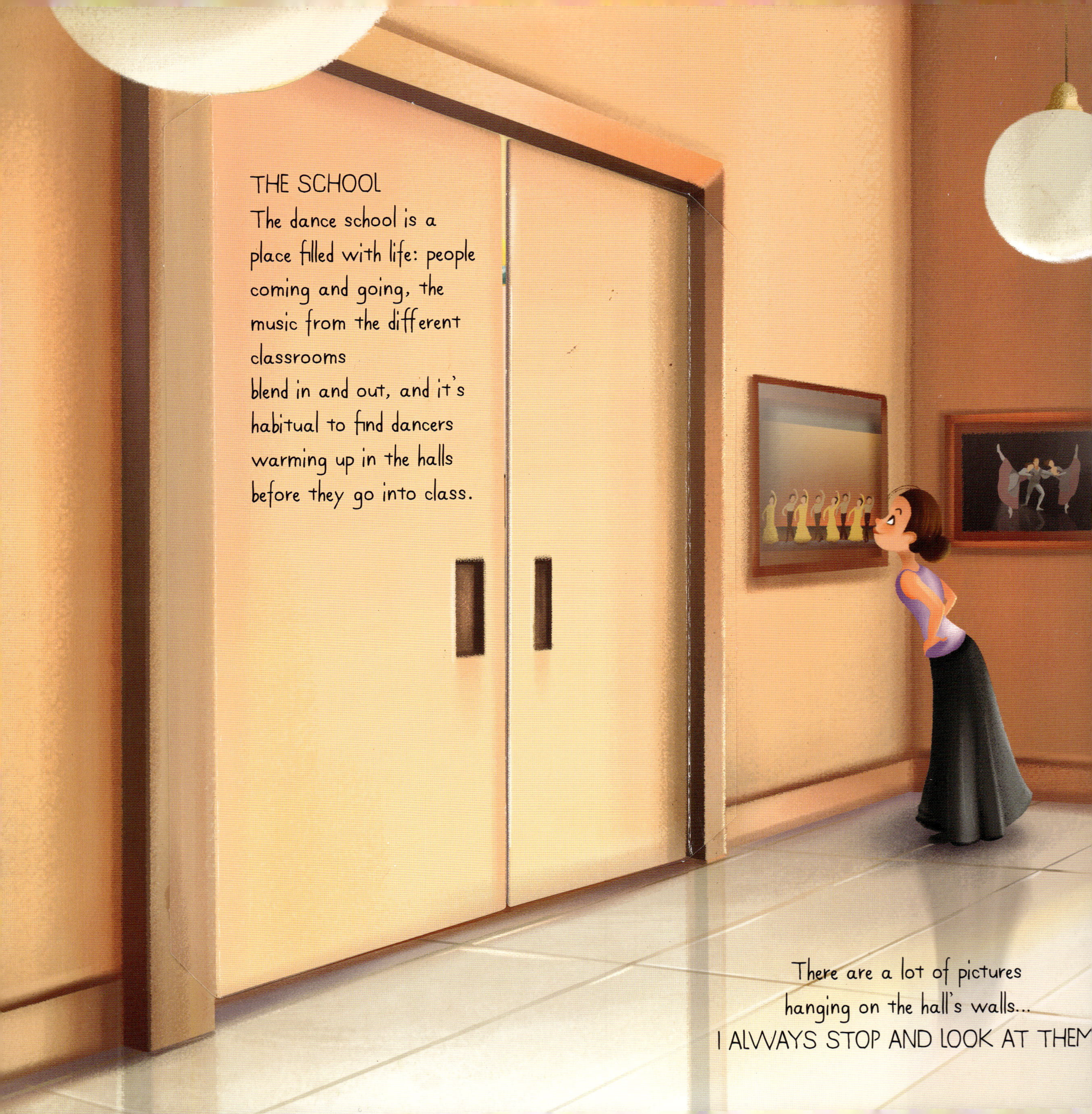

THE SCHOOL

The dance school is a place filled with life: people coming and going, the music from the different classrooms blend in and out, and it's habitual to find dancers warming up in the halls before they go into class.

There are a lot of pictures hanging on the hall's walls...
I ALWAYS STOP AND LOOK AT THEM

In my school, they teach a lot of dance styles: classical ballet, contemporary and modern dance... And other less known Spanish dance styles such as: the «Bolera School,» which is highly artistic and complex and very old tradition; the «danza estilizada, « which is a form of specialized Spanish Dance where there is a freedom of form and choreography; and last , but not least, the Folclore.

THE DANCE CLASSROOM

It's so exciting for me to show you where we rehearse!

It's a big space with wooden floors and a lot of light.

There are bars on two or three sides, and in the other one, a huge mirror where we observe ourselves and correct our movements.

The one indispensable item is the stereo. MUSIC IS THE SOUL OF THE SCHOOL!

Sometimes, the older students leave the door a bit ajar and we can peek in and see what they are doing. I could spend hours and hours just watching them rehearse...

Just seeing how well they dance and listening to Flamenco live, it's a real show!

I WANT TO DANCE LIKE THEM SOME DAY!

CARMEN, MY TEACHER

This is my Flamenco teacher. Her name is Carmen. She is very nice and has a lot of patience. She makes a great effort to teach me everything she knows and help me improve every day. She knows all the steps, and explains to us how to do them, she corrects us...

Sometimes, she calls our attention! Carmen says: « Effort always has a reward,» but, she also reminds us that we have to have to have fun and ENJOY WHILE WE DANCE!

MY CLASS MATES

These are my class mates.. and my best friends in the school!

ANI is the most Flamenco spirited. It's in her family! She feels Flamenco in a very special way.

PATRICIA is the most fun. She always has good ideas and makes up new dances. She's great!

ÓSCAR is always the first one to learn the exercises. He's the only boy in the class, and that's not always easy!

PREPARING FOR CLASS

Remember that class starts at home! Why? Because there you have to prepare carefully your bag and make sure that you have everything you'll need:

I dream of wearing Flamenco gowns and shoes, of all colors and beautiful shapes, but... for the time being, for class we must wear something more simple: a leotard, tights and a rehearsal skirt.

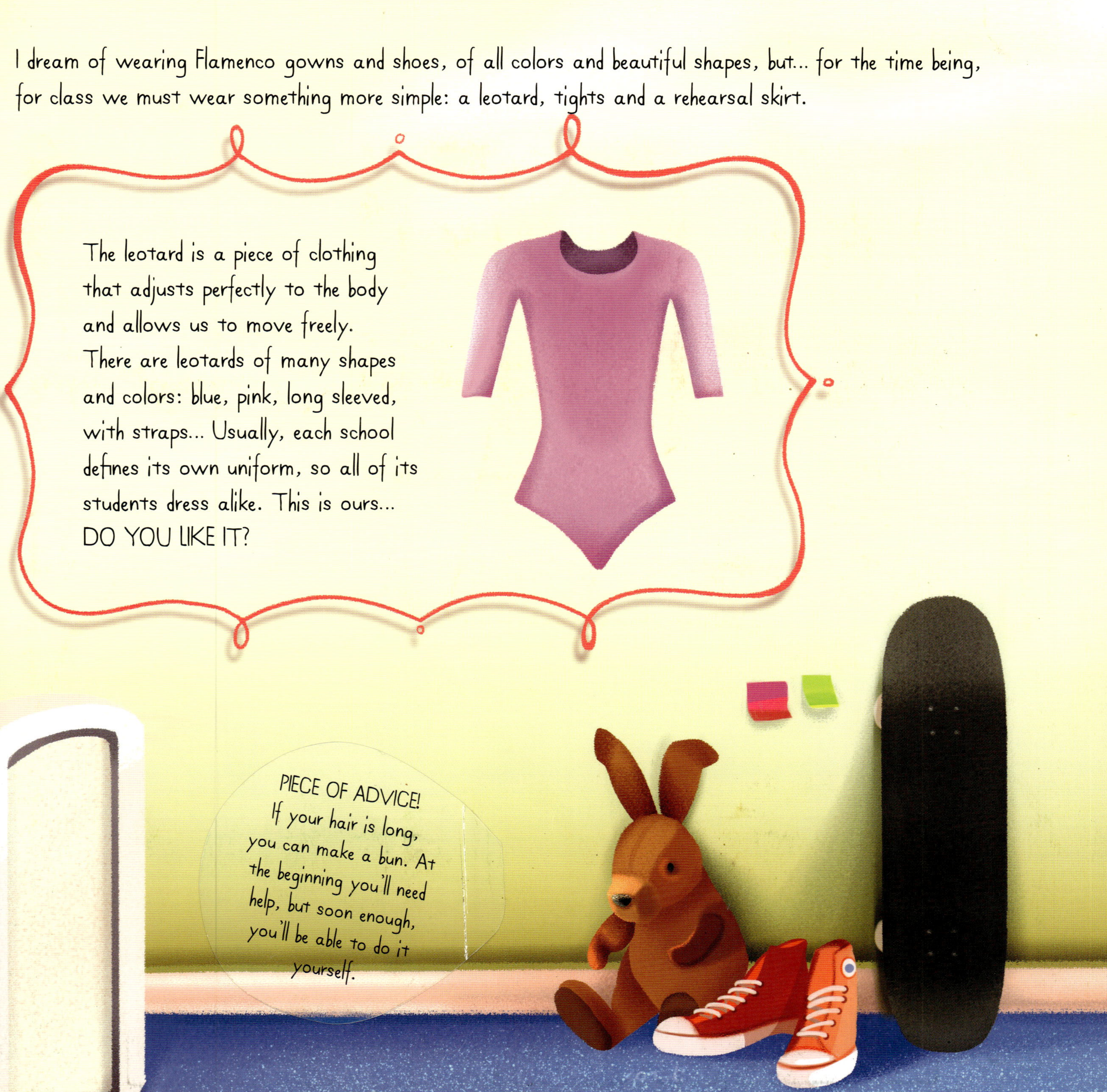

The leotard is a piece of clothing that adjusts perfectly to the body and allows us to move freely. There are leotards of many shapes and colors: blue, pink, long sleeved, with straps... Usually, each school defines its own uniform, so all of its students dress alike. This is ours... DO YOU LIKE IT?

PIECE OF ADVICE! If your hair is long, you can make a bun. At the beginning you'll need help, but soon enough, you'll be able to do it yourself.

CLAPPING!

Clapping is harder than it looks like. Keeping time and marking the different rhythms and beats is an art!

DEAF PALMS

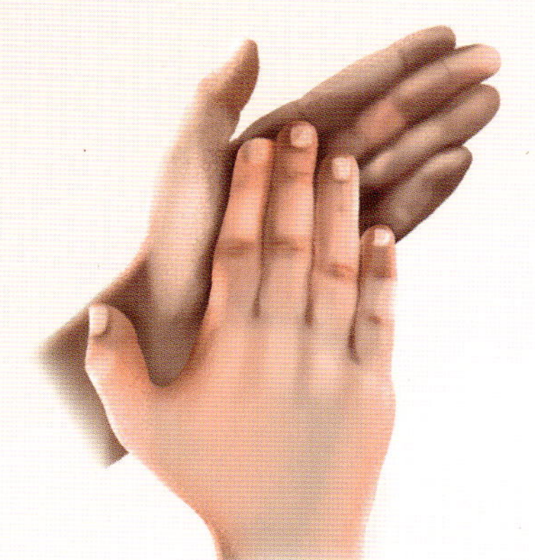

LEARNING HOW TO PLAY THE CASTANETS (OR LITTLE STICKS)

The first thing is to learn how to make the knot right in your castanets.

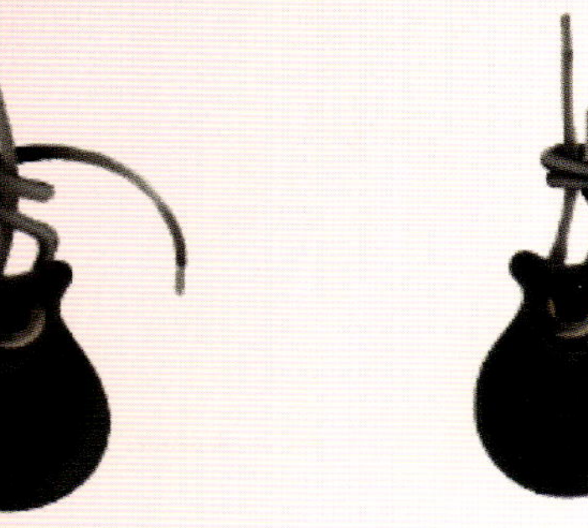

PIECE OF ADVICE!
Try and not leave the strings too long, otherwise, they'll get stuck in the middle of the castanets and they'll bother you.

The castanets have different tones: one is higher and the other lower.
The higher tuned castanet has a mark on the top and always is used in the right hand.
The lower tuned is placed in the left.

The one in the left hand, with the ring and middle fingers together.

The ones in your right hand with four fingers: small, ring, middle and index.

These are the basic castanet touches:

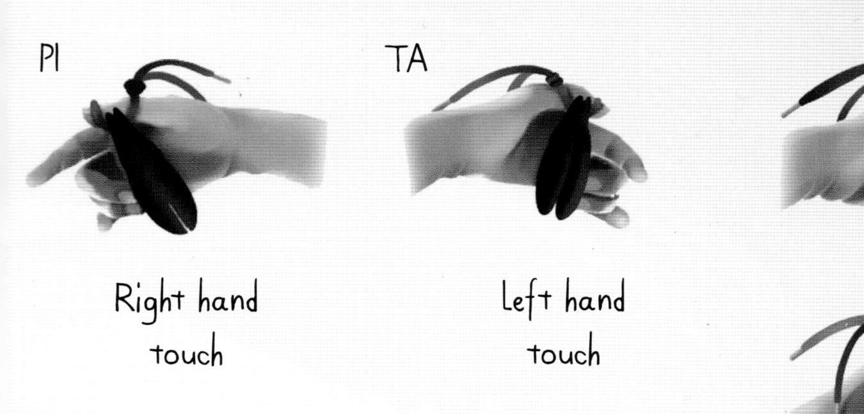

Right hand touch

Left hand touch

PAM

Both hands touch at the same time

RIÁ

Run with the four fingers in the right hand and hit with the left hand

Practice with me these castanet exercises following 3 measure:

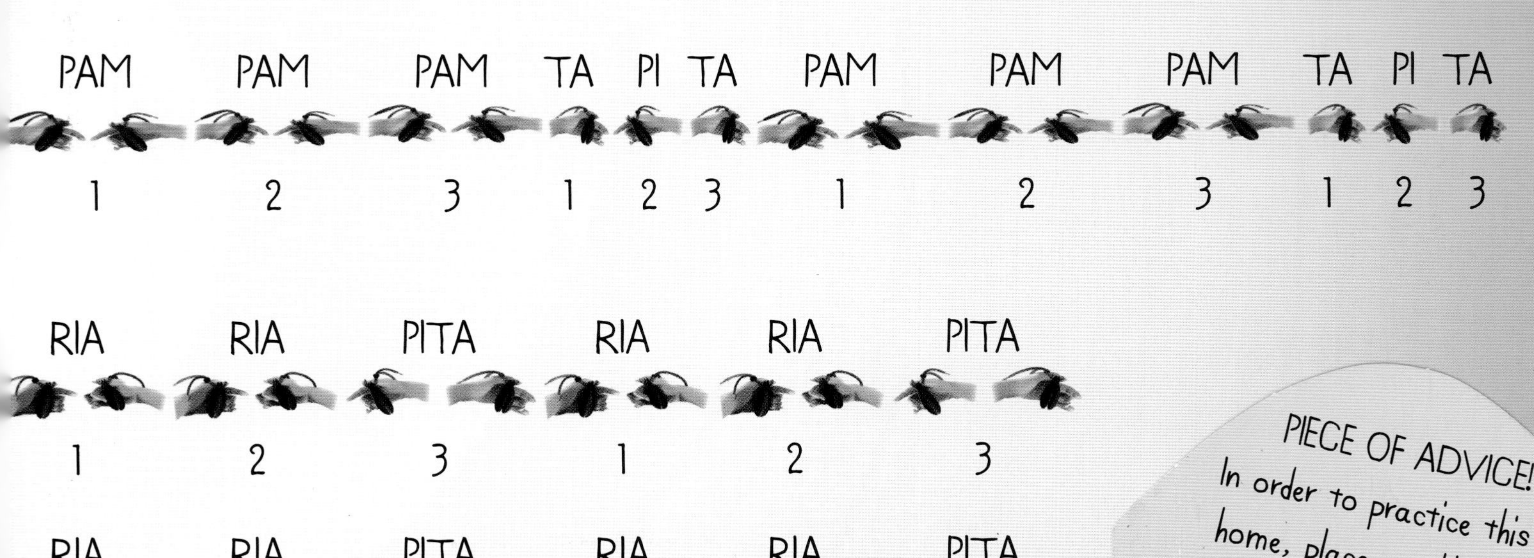

PIECE OF ADVICE!
In order to practice this at home, place a rubber band in the middle of the castanet, this way you'll cushion the sound.

Later on, you'll be able to combine these basic touches to create nuances and very different sounds.

THE MEASURE

Without the measure, or sense of rhythm it's impossible to dance Flamenco.

From your first class on, it's very important to know where the beats are and to respect the rests. Yes, the rests! Even though you may not hear anything, the measure continues in the rests.

The simplest measure is in 3 (like in the Sevillanas and Fandangos:)

(1) 2 3 (1) 2 3 (1) 2 3 (1) 2 3

The 1 is the beat: mark accentuating it with your hands clapping or your foot.

PIECE OF ADVICE! Practice at home listening to Flamenco following the measures with your hands.

Later on, the 4 measure will set in (like the Rumba or the Tangos:)

(1) 2 3 4 (1) 2 3 4 (1) 2 3 4 (1) 2 3 4

The 12 bar measure is the hardest and Flamenco's most characteristic one: «Soleás ,» «Alegrías, «or the «Bulerías.» Here's an example:

1 2 (3) 4 5 (6) 7 (8) 9 (10) 1 (2)

1 2 (3) 4 5 (6) 7 (8) 9 (10) 11 (12)

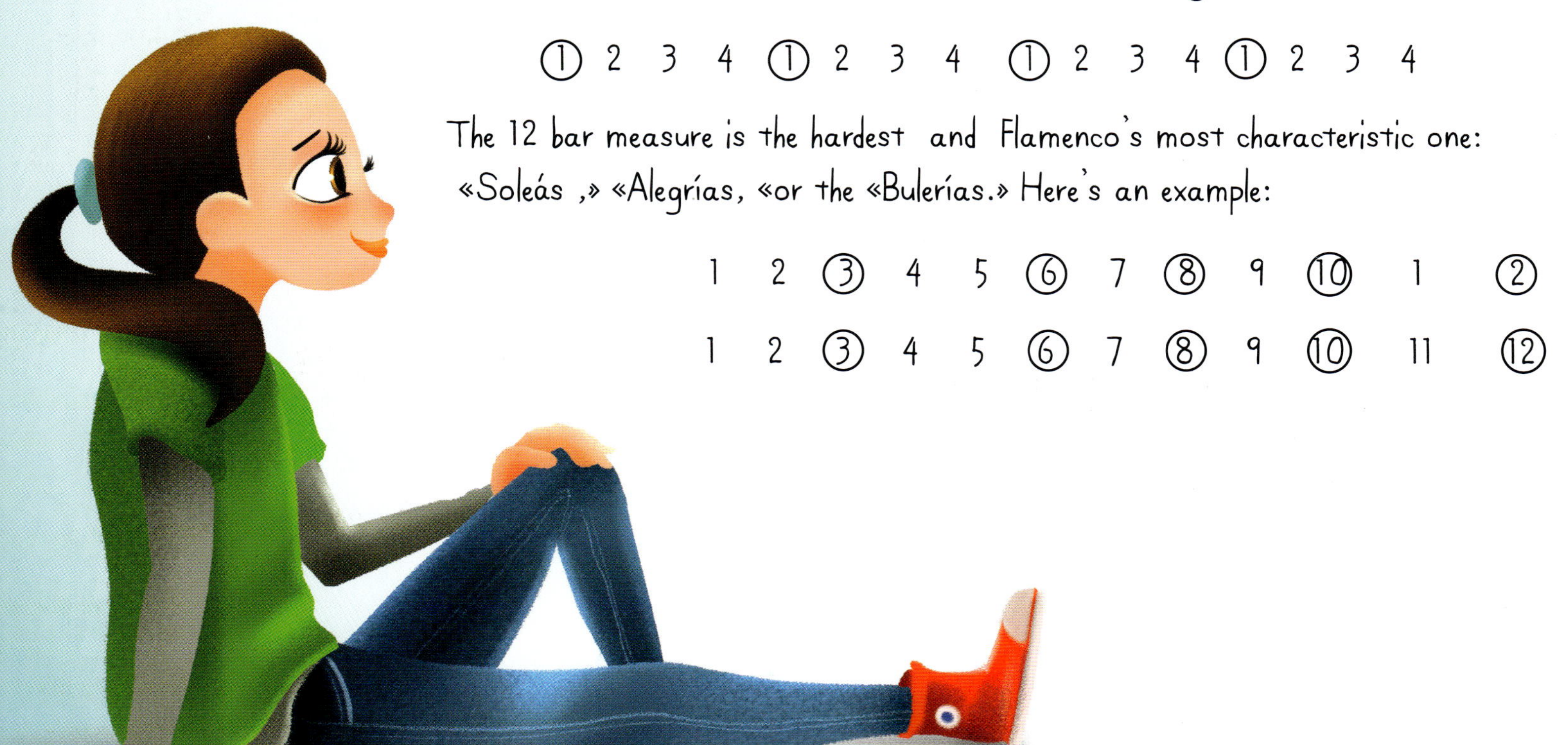

FLAMENCO'S PALOS

Flamenco has an enormous variety of «palos» or styles.

From the most POPULAR ones or simple ones like «SEVILLANAS», or the «FANDANGOS» or the «RUMBA...»

... to the other more complex ones, which you will discover little by little, like the SEGUIRIYA, GUAJIRA, SOLEÁ, or the BULERIAS

Some are very profound and others merrier, but all come from the heart to express different feelings.

We work and practice the different techniques separately. When it comes time to dance, we have to co-ordinate the hands, arms, feet, head... everything! That's what makes the dance harmonious and beautiful. When you manage to do all that, enjoy yourself and put a lot of feeling into it, then, you'll be DANCING FLAMENCO.

GETTING READY FOR THE END OF THE TERM FESTIVAL

When the term is over, dance schools usually prepare a festival to show everything that we have learned. IT'S GREAT!

Thinking about the festival, I have to visit the dance store...

Me, I am going to try on my new flamenco gown. I can't wait!

In these stores you can find everything: costumes of all sorts of colors, shoes, tights, flowers...

I LOVE GOING IN THERE, VISITING THEM
AND SNOOPING AROUND THE WHOLE PLACE!

It's very important to try on the right dress so it's a perfect fit and you feel comfortable in it.

DRESS REHEARSAL... IN THE THEATRE!

Today, at last, you'll have a rehearsal in the theatre where you'll perform in the festival... it's one of my favorite days. Rehearsing in a theatre is very exciting!
Today, you'll practice how to enter and exit the stage in order and silence.
Also, you'll be reminded where you have to stand for the beginning and the curtain calls.
At the end of the dance, the audience will gratify you with may applauses and «oles!!!!!»
We thank these applauses with a curtain call before we leave the stage, it's one of the best moments in the performance.

NOW THE THEATRE SEATS ARE EMPTY, BUT IT'S IMPRESSIVE TO THINK THAT ON THE DAY, THEY WILL BE FILLED WITH PEOPLE WATCHING US DANCE...

Today, at last is the show! I WANT TO DANCE SO MUCH!

I feel a bit strange, as if I had butterflies in my stomach. My mother says it's normal, because I'm a bit nervous, but that it will pass when I see my mates and once I step on the stage. I try to remember my teacher's advice.

If you enjoy while you are dancing, the audience will enjoy it with you.

It's time to listen to the music and get carried away...

The work has been done. Trust yourselves!

Photo Album

It was a very exciting day! The theatre creates a very special ambiance... The dancers and the audience connect and share emotions. IT'S THE MAGIC OF DANCE! I'm not sure what I want to be when I grow up, maybe I'll try and be a professional dancer, or maybe not... but, in the meanwhile, I enjoy dancing a lot and I know that no matter what I do later on, one way or another, I'll always be enjoying and admiring flamenco.

THANK YOU FOR DISCOVERING THIS ENTHRALLING PASSIONATE WORLD WITH ME!

SEE YOU NEXT TIME!